A Reply To **The Greatest Hoax of the Millennium**

WHERE THE TEMPLE WAS NOT LOCATED

BY **BOBBY L. SPARKS, THD**

Where The Temple Was Not Located
by Bobby L. Sparks, ThD

Copyright © 2021 by Tabernacle Ministries

All rights reserved. This book or any portion thereof may not be reproduced, distributed, or transmitted in any form or by any means, including photocopying, recording, or other electronic or mechanical methods, without the express written permission of the publisher or copyright holder except in the case of brief quotations embodied in critical reviews and certain other noncommercial uses permitted by copyright law.

Printed in the United States of America

Winter Haven, FL
www.baptisttrainingcenter.org

Sparks, Bobby -
Where The Temple Was Not Located
Nonfiction > Religion > Antiquities & Archaeology
Nonfiction > Religion > Judaism > History
ISBN 13: 978-1-947598-15-7 (paperback)
ISBN 10: 1-947598-15-5

All scripture quotations are taken from the Holy Bible, King James Version
Painting of Temple by Michael Horton, Jerusalem, Israel

To order more copies of this book contact:
Tabernacle Ministries
3987 CR 3322
Greenville, Texas
903-268-3465
www.oldtestamenttabernacle.com

WHAT THE EXPERTS ARE SAYING:

"In an age of so much misinformation and nonsense, available through the internet and many pseudo-archaeologists promoting their theories without scientific evidence it is refreshing to see a work by Sparks that addresses one of these theories head on and remind readers the necessity for checking their facts. He has compiled a short, well researched, and cogent summary of the evidence for the traditional location of the Second Temple on the Temple Mount along with pointing out the fallacies of Pseudo-archaeologists who want to relocate it."

- David Graves, Ph.D.
University of Aberdeen

"Archaeology is a slow and arduous process, and our publications pass through a rigorous peer-review gauntlet. This protects the public from the type of misinformation that unqualified or unscrupulous "researchers" peddle under the guise of new discoveries. Currently, the most egregious example of misinformation is that the first and second Jewish temples stood in the city of David, rather than on the Temple Mount. Bobby Sparks has distilled irrefutable evidence that the Jewish temples stood on the Temple Mount. Rarely does a week pass that I am not asked about this issue. Going forward, I plan to point such inquirers to this booklet for an accurate and succinct treatment of this topic."

- Dr. Scott Stripling, Ph.D.
Director of Excavations for the Associates for Biblical Research at Khirbet el-Maqatir and Shiloh, Israel and the provost at The Bible Seminary in Katy (Houston), Texas.

"Historically the location of the Jewish Temple has never been in question. Archaeologists have no doubt that the Temple was on the historic site of Mt. Moriah identified with the modern Temple Mount. However, a recent sensationalists theory has upset the uniformed Christian community, causing some to question pastors and scholars who maintain the historic view. Fortunately, Dr. Sparks has answered this theory with biblical, archaeological and historical evidence that affirms the historic view enabling concerned Christians to settle this current controversy."

- Randall Price, Ph.D.
Distinguished Research Professor of Biblical & Judaic Studies
Rawlings School of Divinity, Liberty University
Co-Director, Qumran Cave Excavation Project, Dead Sea, Israel

" I have refuted the Temple in the City of David many times in my blog, which the followers of Martin & Co. apparently don't read or refer to. Cornuke completely ignores my book The Quest in his bibliography for it clearly would destroy his theory. Hopefully you, as a pastor, will have more success among the Christian community in the USA. These weird, and almost anti-semitic ideas, not only discredit Christian believers, but also make a mockery of dearly held Jewish convictions that the Temple stood on the Temple Mount."

- Leen Ritmeyer, Ph.D.
University of Manchester, England; Ritmeyer Archaeological Design

This booklet is not intended to be an exhaustive research on every detail of the arguments for the location of the Temple. It merely submits the main evidence sufficient enough to debunk a false premise about the Temple's location in the old City of David.

The final outcome of the issue is not so important. It really does not matter where the Temple was located. It alone is not basis for a division in fellowship.

The real issue, in spite of Martin's theory being so erroneously presented, is that people believe it hook, line and sinker without study and research. Thick books have been written, and videos with persuasive speakers, articles, drawings, etc. fill bookstores and the internet. Their theory permeates American theology. We need to be more like the Bereans who "... were more noble than those in Thessalonica, in that they received the word with all readiness of mind, and searched the scriptures daily, whether those things were so" (Acts 17:11).

If people are so easily convinced of this new teaching without examination, they will most likely follow "every wind of doctrine, by the sleight of men, and cunning craftiness, whereby they lie in wait to deceive;" (Eph. 4:14). The important thing, in this case, is not where the Temple is located, but how quickly people will believe gross error without scrutiny.

- Author

**This study will be considered
under the following topics:**

Martin's Theory Examined
Page 5

Biblical Evidence
Page 13

The Tower of Antonia and the Tenth Legion
Page 15

Archaeological Evidence
Page 20

Martin's Theory Examined

There have always been discussions about the location of the Temple on Temple Mount. Additionally, there have been suggestions that the Temple was originally positioned in other locations. In the past, these suggested locations did not gain much attention. However, in recent years, the idea that the Temple was located in the old City of David and not on Temple Mount has gained popularity, especially in America. The first to popularize the view was Ernest L. Martin in his book, *The Temples that Jerusalem Forgot*. After Martin's death, Robert Cornuke promotes the idea in his book *Temple* with the caption "Could History Be So Stunningly Wrong?" Followed by Mike M. Joseph's book, *Jerusalem's Temple Mount: The Hoax of The Millennium*! Addentionally, Ken Klein in his documentary, "Jerusalem and the Lost Temple of the Jews," continues to circulate the claim. Since then, many articles and videos have surfaced filling the Internet with the same allegation. People have accepted these writings and videos without scrutiny, and the concept has become popular among many Christian leaders.

A thorough examination of the facts will likely cause one to see the fallacy of these arguments. The weakness of this proposal lies in the fact that it consists mainly of Ernest Martin's personal interpretation of both the Scriptural passages and historical evidence as well as that of various writers who have taken up and advocate his position. These authors are guilty of taking Scriptures out of context and applying yet-to-be-fulfilled prophesies to ancient events. They misquote the historians, hoping that readers do not validate their writings. They leave out pertinent information and in some cases, they contradict their own writings. Some examples are as follows:

1) Mistaken Location of the Camp of the Tenth Legion

Martin claims that the traditional Temple Mount was actually the location of the Fortress Antonia rather than that of Herod's Temple. He further maintains that the Temple was located farther south in the old City of David. His allegation refutes all scholarly, historical and archaeological claims that Herod's Temple was located on the traditional Temple Mount.

According to Martin, he was the first to bring to light the true location of the Temple. He argued the Temple was located in the old City of David, and the Roman Tenth Legion occupied what most believe is the traditional Temple site, on or near the Muslim Dome of the Rock. Martin said, "There is no proof whatever that the Tenth Legion had its camp in the Upper City or anywhere in the west part of Jerusalem" (Martin, pg 47).

Cornuke concurs that the camp of the Roman Tenth Legion was located in the Fortress Antonia atop the traditional Temple Mount and nowhere else in the city. Cornuke wrote, "There is not one shred of evidence that a huge Roman fort has ever been found anywhere in Jerusalem" (Cornuke, pg 48).

However, the error of these statements is demonstrated by the huge archaeological uncovering of the camp of the Tenth Legion surrounding the Crown Plaza Hotel in Jerusalem in the western part of the city, exactly as previous historians had asserted. The front courtyard and streets around the hotel have become an archaeological dig. Thousands of artifacts of the Tenth Legion have been uncovered. These are the types of artifacts that would have been found on the Temple mount had they camped there. The absence of such artifacts on the Temple Mount location repudiates the claim that the Tenth Legion camped there.

2) Incorrect Application of Future Events

Martin quotes Joel 3:18 which says "… and a fountain shall come forth of the house of the LORD" (Martin, pg 301). The problem is, Martin, it's the wrong Temple! Joel 3:18 is speaking of the Millennial Temple where there will be major changes in the size, shape, and worship from that of Herod's Temple. You cannot determine what Herod's Temple was like from reading about the Temple to be built during the Millennium. Mr. Martin erroneously claims the first name for Jerusalem was Migdal Eder from Micah 4:8 (Martin, pg 289). Migdal Eder is clearly Bethlehem and the birthplace of Jesus (Micha 5:2). Martin draws unsubstantiated statements out of thin air.

3) Based on Imagination

Martin and Cornuke's drawings and diagrams are not the result of archaeological research and findings but rather the result of a flawed interpretation of the Bible, fraudulent research, and distorted historical claims. None of these men have archaeological training and experience, and their theological opinions are to the far left of mainstream Christianity. Not one reputable Israeli archaeological scholar endorses their view.

4) Overstating the Facts

Regarding the destruction of the Temple in the City of David, Martin asserts (and his colleagues agree with him), "It was so destroyed that modern archaeologists will not be able to discover any remnants of it within the confines of its former site. They will not find even its foundation stones that were once strongly positioned in place" (Martin, pg 5). This statement is nothing more than supposition and is convenient to bolstering his position. This is his excuse to explain away the fact that no archaeological evidence for the Temple can be found in the old City of David even though he insists it was located there.

To build a massive Temple in the City of David would have required major excavations. If the ruins of the earlier civilizations are undisturbed as they are, would that not be archaeological evidence that no Temple was built over the site? Are we so foolish to believe that every single stone, column, timber, every piece of the Temple was removed out of the City of David without disturbing the remains of David's palace as well as other civilizations? There are no remains and artifacts of the Temple in the rubble of the old City of David. However, there are archaeological finds and evidence on the traditional Temple Mount site which indicate the Temple once sat there. These archaeological items are not being unearthed in the ruins of the old City of David.

5) Adding What Is NOT There

In all the material offered by the proponents of the Temple being in the City of David, it is upheld that there was a 600-foot bridge connecting the southwest corner of Antonia to the northwest corner of the Temple Complex. Ernest Martin said, "As clear as Josephus could make it, he stated that the distance between the southern wall of Fort Antonia and the northern wall of the Temple was one *stade*. See *War* II. 2, 6" (Martin, pg. 413, footnotes).

Robert Cornuke wrote:

> It seems that Josephus wrote that the distance between the Temple and the Roman fort was exactly one stade (approximately 600 feet). In truth Josephus recorded that King Herod built two side-by-side bridges (*Jewish Wars* VI 2, 6; II 15, 6) connecting the gap between the Temple and the Roman Fort (refer to Cornfeld translation as well as *The Temples that Jerusalem Forgot*, p. 413). (Cornuke, pg 61)

Do they think we will not read the Josephus references? There is no mention of a stade and two bridges in these references of Josephus. Later in this book, this matter will be discussed.

6) Erroneous Definitions

There are countless problems with this theory. In the quoted references of Josephus, there is not one single hint of two bridges, much less bridges that run parallel for some 600 feet. Josephus used the term *cloisters* repeatedly, which has the same meaning of colonnades. His description of the Temple Complex is that these colonnades ran around the perimeter of the complex. The Tower of Antonia was built at the intersection of the colonnades on the north and west corner of the complex. They are not bridges, and nowhere are they called bridges in any writings except those of Martin and Cornuke who have deceptively changed the meaning of *cloister* to *bridge*. Even though they claim Josephus said the bridges were the length of a stade, there is no mention of a stade in the Josephus/historical reference.

A picture of a portico or colonnade similar to what was around the Temple complex perimeter. The outside wall was enclosed and columns held a roof under which people could gather. A bridge could have such columns, but it would have to have terminology identifying it as a bridge. The mere colonnade or portico does not identify as a bridge.

Secondly, Martin had to incorrectly define *cloister* and add two bridges to accommodate his distorted view of the Fortress Antonia to go down into the City of David to the Temple Complex. His interpretation presents a new problem. He claims the Temple Complex as remodeled by Herod was some 750 feet in each direction (Martin, footnotes, pg 253). He said that the southeast corner of the complex covered the Gihon Spring. If you begin at Gihon Spring and go north 750 feet, you do not have an additional 600 feet of space for the bridges.

According to satellite images and maps, the distance from Gihon Spring to the southern wall of the traditional mount is approximately 804 feet. This means that to place the southeast corner of the Temple over Gihon Spring, the Temple complex would come within 50 feet of the southern wall. Not only is there not room for a 600 foot bridge, the Temple alone would barely fit. Just look at Martin's distorted picture of the fortress and Temple complex. He reduces the square Temple complex to a narrow, rectangular shape to make room for the two 600-foot bridges.

7) An Inflexible Interpretation

Martin and his colleagues are totally inflexible in their interpretation of the location of Zion. While they are correct in some of their views, they are adamant that their opinion is the only correct interpretation. Their argument is that the City of David is Mount Zion and that the Temple was built on Mount Zion; therefore, the Temple had to be built in the City of David, end of discussion.

While Mount Zion does refer to the city of Jerusalem, it is not the physical location that is the emphasis of the term. Mount Zion does not refer to a mountain range on which the city sits, but it refers to the city that sits on the hill, namely Jerusalem. Even then, city limits expand and the city name remains the same.

"Rashi identifies the location as the source of 'joy' mentioned in the Psalm as the Temple complex and all involved in making atonement. In the New Testament, Mount Zion is used metaphorically to refer to the heavenly Jerusalem, God's holy, eternal city (Heb. 12:22; Rev. 14:1)." (Menachem Davis, ed., pg 128). Earthly Jerusalem is a type of heavenly Jerusalem; earthly Mount Zion is a type of heavenly Mount Zion. As Jerusalem expanded, so did Mount Zion.

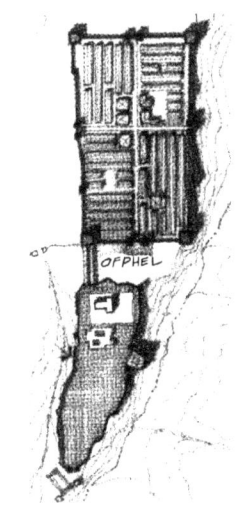

These proponents have difficulty explaining the fact that Solomon brought the Ark of the Covenant "out of" the city of David to the newly constructed Temple site. (I Kings 8:1, 2 Chron. 5:2).

The above diagram reflects the position of David Cornuke. Notice the ophel between the fortress and Temple. His drawing contradicts what he has in writing.

There is therefore no contradiction between the Temple being located in Zion, that is Jerusalem, and yet being placed just north of the City of David on Mount Moriah.

8) Contradictory Conclusions

Ernest Martin quotes several sources in an attempt to prove that the southeast corner of the Temple covered Gihon Spring and that the spring was within the Temple confines. While it is true that the Gihon was the only natural spring, it is not true that it was the only source of water.

Martin wrote, "David actually pitched the Tent for the Ark (called a 'Tabernacle' in the King James Version) on a terrace region directly above and within the immediate of [sic] view of the Gihon Spring" (Martin, pg 295). There is no historical or Biblical record of where David placed the Tabernacle, nor can Martin be certain of its location.

TOP of the Ophel (Diagram A)

Martin goes on to say, "Solomon (after building the Temple) simply moved the Ark up to the **TOP OF THE OPHEL HILL** to his new Temple located a little higher above the Gihon Spring." (Martin, pg 296, emphasis mine)

BELOW the Ophel (Diagram B)

Then a few pages later he contradicts himself, "This is why Solomon felt it incumbent to follow David and position the original Temple directly over the Gihon Spring which was near the northern foot of the original mount Zion (the akra) and **JUST BELOW THE OPHEL SUMMIT**" (emphasis mine). (Martin, pg 299). In the selfsame paragraph Mr. Martin writes about Warren's shaft and states, "It was constructed to reach the Gihon **FROM THE OPHEL SUMMIT (where the Temple was built).** (emphasis mine)

CENTER of the City (Diagram C)

It gets even more contradictory. On page 275 of his book, Ernest Martin writes, "The Tabernacle was indeed pitched directly in the center of the encampment of the tribes of Israel. In order to duplicate this design, Solomon's Temple was also placed in the *center* of Jerusalem, **IN THE *CENTER* OF THE CRESCENT SHAPED RIDGE**."

Earnest Martin's Three Locations of the Temple in the City of David

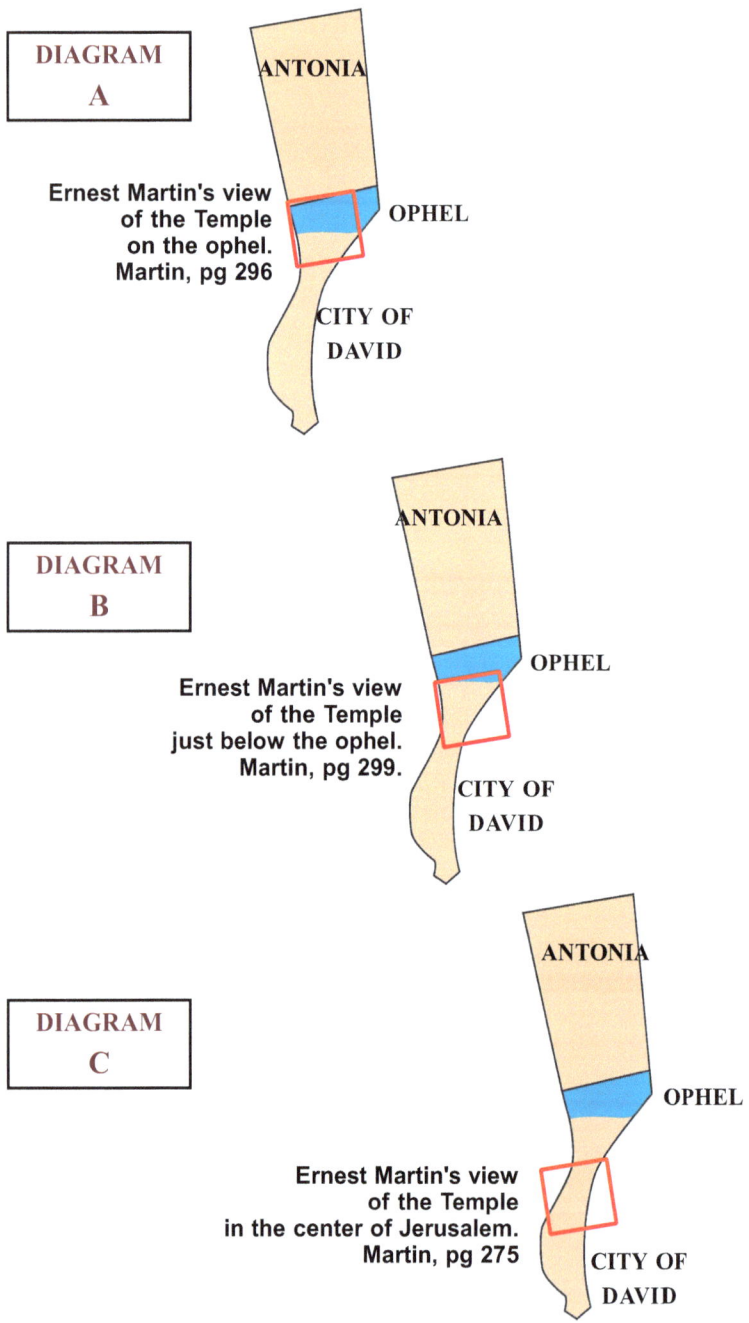

Biblical Evidence

1). The Threshing Floor of Araunah

To stay the plague that God brought upon Israel for their disobedience, God told David to purchase the threshing floor from Araunah and make a sacrifice. It is recorded: "And Gad came that day to David, and said unto him, Go up, rear an altar unto the LORD in the threshingfloor of Araunah the Jebusite. And David, according to the saying of Gad, went up as the LORD commanded." (2 Samuel 24:18-19) Notice that David "went up" from Jerusalem to take possession of the threshing floor. 1 Chronicles 21:18 records: "Then the angel of the LORD commanded Gad to say to David, that David should go up, and set up an altar unto the LORD in the threshingfloor of Ornan the Jebusite." Likewise David was told by the angel to "go up" to set up the altar. 2 Chronicles 3:1 establishes the location of the Temple to be in the same location as the threshing floor. "Then Solomon began to build the house of the LORD at Jerusalem in mount Moriah, where the LORD appeared unto David his father, in the place that David had prepared in the threshingfloor of Ornan the Jebusite."

2). The Location of the Ark of the Covenant.

Once the Temple was completed, Solomon brought the Ark of the Covenant up from the City of David to the Temple location. "Then Solomon assembled the elders of Israel, and all the heads of the tribes, the chief of the fathers of the children of Israel, unto Jerusalem, to bring up the ark of the covenant of the LORD out of the city of David, which is Zion." (2 Chronicles 5:2) The Ark of the Covenant was brought "up … **out of the city of David**" to the new Temple location. There is no greater affirmation than this passage that the Temple was not built in the old City of David, and those who say it was are arguing in the face of God.

3). Solomon's Palace and the House of Pharaoh's Daughter

Solomon built his private palace in the vicinity of the Temple. Next to his palace, Solomon built a house for his Egyptian wife, the daughter of Pharaoh. "And Solomon made affinity with Pharaoh king of Egypt, and took Pharaoh's daughter, and brought her into the city of David, until he had made an end of building his own house, and the house of the LORD, and the wall of Jerusalem round about." (1 Kings 3:1) Then Solomon built a special palace for his Egyptian wife. "Solomon made also an house for Pharaoh's daughter, whom he had taken to wife, like unto this porch." (1 Kings 7:8) Once her house was finished, she moved from the City of David to her new home next to Solomon's palace. "But Pharaoh's daughter came up out of the city of David unto her house which Solomon had built for her ..." (1 Kings 9:24; 2 Chron. 8:11). Obviously, the Temple, Solomon's palace, and the home of Pharaoh's daughter were not located in the City of David.

4). Additional Consideration

In addition to the Biblical points, Josephus adds one more bit of information, "Now this Temple, as I have already said, was built upon a strong hill." (*Wars of the Jews.* V 5, 1, pg 554). The hill was the area north of the old City of David upon which stood the threshing floor of Araunah, and where Abram nearly offered Isaac. The mountain ridge north of the old city was higher in elevation, and this is where the threshing floor was located, and this is where Solomon was directed to build the Temple. Josephus' position is harmonious with the Biblical record.

The Tower of Antonia and The Tenth Legion

Josephus describes cloisters (colonnades) around the perimeter of the Temple complex. These cloisters were thirty cubits wide (45 feet), and the pillars were twenty-five cubits high (38 feet) (*Wars of the Jews.* V 5, 2, pg 554). Josephus describes these cloisters as surrounding the outermost court of the Temple complex.

Josephus then goes on to describe the location of the Tower of Antonia:

> Now, as to the tower of Antonia, it was situated at the corner of two cloisters of the court of the Temple; of that on the west and that on the north; it was erected upon a rock of fifty cubits in height, and was on a great precipice; it was the work of king Herod, wherein he demonstrated his natural magnanimity (*War of the Jews,* V 5, 8, pg 56).

He goes on to describe it as a beautiful structure with four distinct towers at its four corners. The tower on the south-east corner was seventy cubits high (105 feet). The purpose of this high tower was to enable the Roman garrison to look into the Temple courtyard and spy on the activities of the Jews. The Tower of Antonia was originally built by the Hasmoneans. Josephus describes it this way:

> Now on the north side [of the Temple] was built a citadel, whose walls were square, and strong, and of extraordinary firmness. This citadel was built by the kings of the Asamonean race, who were also high priests before Herod, and they called it the Tower, in which were reposited the vestments of the high priest, which the high priest only put on at the time when he was to offer sacrifice. But for the tower itself, when Herod the king of the Jews had fortified it more firmly than before, in order to secure and guard the Temple, he gratified

Antonius, who was his friend, and the Roman ruler, and then gave it the name of the Tower of Antonia." (*Antiquities of the Jews.* XV 11, 4, pg 335)

In 35 BC, King Herod rebuilt the tower of the Hasmoneans into a strong fortress to protect the Temple complex. He renamed it after Herod's friend Marcus Antonius. Historians claim the Antonia Fortress was garrisoned with about 600 Roman soldiers, who watched over the Temple courts in order to preserve order. The Bible spoke about the Antonia Fortress as a castle (Acts 21:37).

There are several problems historically with recent writers claiming that what is called the Temple Mount today was incorrectly identified, and that it was actually the Tower of Antonia. First, the Hasmoneans did not build a 36-acre complex to house the priest's garments. In order to access the Temple, Titus needed a clear path. Josephus told us, "... Titus gave orders to his soldiers that were with him to dig up the foundations of the tower of Antonia, and make him a ready passage for his army to come up" (*Wars of the Jews,* VI 2, 1, pg 574). Later, Josephus wrote that the Romans destroyed a large section of the Tower of Antonia to the bedrock in seven days. "In the meantime, the rest of the Roman army had, in seven days' time, overthrown [some] foundations of the tower of Antonia, and had made a ready and broad way to the Temple" (*Wars of the Jews,* VI 2, 7, pg 576).

The traditional site of the Temple Mount was not destroyed on any side to the bedrock and certainly could not have been done in seven days. In an effort to explain this away, Martin said, "But Titus changed his mind ..." (Martin pg 17; footnote, pg 13). However, there is no record that Titus changed his mind, nor any evidence of the same. Furthermore, if the Tower of Antonia was 600 feet (2 football fields) away from the Temple complex, why would they have to tear down some adjoining walls to gain access to the Temple?

Martin and his followers have created a model for the Tower of Antonia and claimed that it occupied the space traditionally believed to be the Temple Mount. They maintain that it was the camp of the Tenth Legion Roman army. They also allege that as many as 5,000 soldiers with a support group of the same, as many as 10,000 occupied that hill. Elaborate drawings, detailed designs, exhaustive arguments, and meticulous comparisons are all in vain. The Hasmoneans built it; Herod enlarged it; but the Tenth Legion never occupied it. Although the date of original construction is not known, Herod began remodeling and enlarging Antonia in 35 BC. The span of time from 35 BC to AD 70 is 105 years. In the 105 years of its existence, the Tenth Legion of the Roman army never as much as spent the night there. During the time of Herod, a garrison of about 600 soldiers were stationed there, and that is a far cry from the 5,000 members of the Tenth Legion and their additional support group making 10,000 occupants.

The event that triggered the destruction of Jerusalem was the rebellion of the Jews and their taking over the Antonia Fortress. If as many as 10,000 Romans occupied the site, it must have been some battle that the Jews were able to assault the fortress and drive out a Roman Legion. The first thing General Titus was required to do was to take back the fortress from the rebels.

The intellectual dishonesty of Martin and Cornuke is staggering. Cornuke wrote:

> However, per Dr. Martin, there has been a blatant mistranslation of Josephus' words in Williamson and the Loeb editions by Thackeray. That translation of Josephus is said to use the word *cohort* in describing the amount of soldiers at the fort — which would make for a much smaller contingent of about 480 or so men. The big question that begs to be asked here is why did a translator change the correct rendering of *tagma*, which was approximately 6,000 soldiers? (Cornuke, pg 48).

Apparently they thought that no one will look up *tagma* in a Greek dictionary? *Strong's Exhaustive Concordance* defines *tagma* simply as "something orderly in arrangement (a troop), i.e. (figuratively) a series or succession -- order. (*Strong's,* 5001). The only time the verse is used in the Bible, it is translated "order."

1 Corinthians 15:23, "But every man in his own order: Christ the firstfruits; afterward they that are Christ's at his coming. But every man in his own order: Christ the firstfruits; afterward they that are Christ's at his coming." The word does not define a cohort nor a legion; it only means that whatever number is represented, it is in order.

Unfortunately, Ernest Martin and his colleagues did not do their homework. General Titus brought the Tenth Legion of the Roman army into Jerusalem in AD 70 in order to put down the rebellion. By the time they arrived, Antonia was 105 years old. The Tenth Legion put up their camp on the Mount of Olives. Once they overtook Antonia, they moved on to the Temple fortress, and after conquering both Antonia and the Temple complex, they destroyed a major part of Antonia to the foundation. Then Titus moved down to the southern city and razed it (*Wars of the Jews,* VII 7, 2, pg 585).

Jerusalem was besieged by four Roman legions. The 5th, 12th, and 15th Legions settled on the western side of the city. The Tenth Legion was positioned on the Mount of Olives. The Tenth Legion entered from the north in Galilee and camped the first winter in Acre. Then they moved to Caesarea to spend the next summer. After that, they came down the Jordan Valley to Jericho, conquered Qumran, and settled in for another winter. From Jericho, they came up to Jerusalem. Once the war was over, the first three legions left the country, and the Tenth Legion remained in Israel for cleaning up the last remaining rebels, Masada being the last stronghold.

The Tenth Legion settled in Jerusalem on the western part of the city and remained there for nearly 150 years until they were removed and integrated with other legions. They took occupancy of the ground where the other three Legions camped. No Roman Legion historically occupied the parcel of ground traditionally known as the Temple Mount. The camp of the Tenth Legion has been unearthed in the western part of the city of Jerusalem. The area is filled with thousands of artifacts including sandals, spears, swords, arrows, utensils, etc. belonging to the Tenth Legion. All such Tenth Legion artifacts are absent from the Temple Mount area of Jerusalem.

When referring to the bridges, Robert Cornuke writes:

> "It seems that Josephus wrote that the distance between the temple and the Roman fort was exactly one stade (approximately 600 feet). Josephus recorded that King Herod built two side-by-side bridges (Jewish Wars, VI, 2, 6, and II, 15, 6) connecting the gap between the temple and the Roman fort (refer to Cornfield translation as well as The Temples that Jerusalem Forgot, p. 413). (Cornuke, pg 61).

However, Josephus actually wrote, "But for the seditions, they were afraid lest Florus should come again, and get possession of the temple, through Antonia; so they got immediately upon those cloisters of the temple that joined to Antonia, and cut them down" (*Wars of the Jews*, II 15, 6). In the other reference of Josephus, there is not one single word about two side-by-side bridges. There is no mention of two bridges, neither is there a hint of two bridges being one stade (600 feet long). The very best we can make of this is faux history.

FACT CHECK:
The entire City of David is estimated to be about 12-13 acres. The Temple mount complex of 500 square cubits at 18 inches encompasses 12.92 acres. Figuring 500 square cubits at 20.67 inches per cubit, it encompasses 17 acres, considerably larger than the city itself.

Archaeological Evidence

1). Trumpeting Stone

Josephus records that one of the battles took place on the southwest corner of the Temple area, "...where one of the priests stood of course, and gave a signal beforehand, with a trumpet, at the beginning of every seventh day, in the evening twilight, as also at the evening when the day was finished" (*Wars of the Jews.* IV 9, 12, pg 543).

The trumpeting stone was said by Josephus to be on the southwest corner of the Temple complex. The Romans destroyed the Temple and pushed the debris off the mount to the ground below. The trumpeting stone was buried in this debris until 1967. It was discovered at the southwest base of the traditional Temple Mount and ***not*** in the old City of David. This archaeological find is more than sufficient evidence to prove the traditional Temple mount was in fact the location of the Temple.

The original trumpeting stone is in the Israeli Museum.

2). Gihon Spring and Jebusite Structure

Excavations in the area of Gihon Spring have uncovered remains of the Jebusite structure that had been built around the spring area. According to Ernest Martin and those holding to his theory, the southeast corner of the Temple covered the spring, and the spring was "inside" the Temple. They further assert that this corner was the pinnacle of the Temple standing 450 feet high.

The Jebusites built a massive spring tower to fortify the city's water system and allow the people of Jerusalem to safely access fresh water in times of siege. The foundation to this tower is still in place. Had Solomon built an immense 450 foot corner wall on the site, it would have required that he excavate to bedrock in order to build the wall around the spring. Archaeologically, the Jebusite tower base is still intact and there is no evidence that a massive 450 foot wall stood in the place.

3). Hezekiah's Tunnel

When the Assyrians were approaching Jerusalem, King Hezekiah dug a tunnel from Gihon Spring to the pool of Siloam. 2 Chronicles 32:2-4 reads, "And when Hezekiah saw that Sennacherib was come, and that he was purposed to fight against Jerusalem, He took counsel with his princes and his mighty men to stop the waters of the fountains which were without the city: and they did help him. So there was gathered much people together, who stopped all the fountains, and the brook that ran through the midst of the land, saying, Why should the kings of Assyria come, and find much water?" 2 Kings 20:20 sums it up: "And the rest of the acts of Hezekiah, and all his might, and how he made a pool, and a conduit, and brought water **into the city,** are they not written in the book of the chronicles of the kings of Judah?" (emphasis mine)

Hezekiah's tunnel brings the water from Gihon Spring "into the city."

The Temple was built long before Hezekiah, and if the southeast corner of the Temple covered Gihon Spring, why did Hezekiah build a tunnel to bring the "fountains which were **without the city**" "**into the city**?" Hezekiah's tunnel is still intact until this day to give witness that the Temple was *not* in the City of David.

4). The Size of the Temple Complex and the City of David

If Ernest Martin and his followers are right, the massive Temple complex would have covered up the greater part of the City of David. Robert Cornuke acknowledges in writing that the Temple complex was some 750 feet square. His diagram contradicts his writings. He said that the southeast corner of the Temple covered Gihon Spring and that the spring was "within" the Temple.

Cornuke makes two major mistakes. First, he deflates the Temple to make it fit in the diagram. Secondly, Cornuke falsely inflates the width of the city to help make it larger than it is so as to fit the Temple inside the walls. The ancient city had a maximum width of less than 400 feet at its widest point. The minimum Temple complex was 750 feet wide, making it the Temple complex almost 350 feet wider than the widest part of the city. In addition, between the Temple complex and the fortress, there would not have been room for a 600 foot bridge.

Leen Ritmeyer has well established in his book *The Quest, Revealing the Temple Mount in Jerusalem,* pg 173, that the cubit measured 20.67 inches rather than the traditional 18 inches. This means Martin and Cornuke's Temple complex would be some 861 feet square.

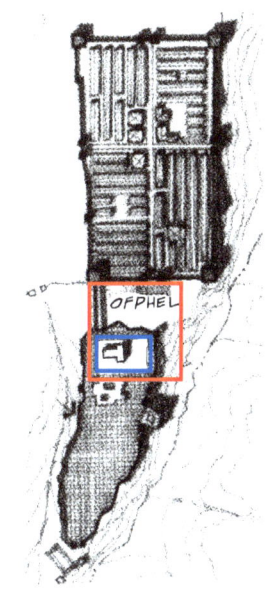

Notice the miniature temple sketch in Robert Cornuke's book, pg 144 attempting to make it fit.

The blue line reveals Cornuke's Temple complex in the diagram, but the red line reflects his written claims as to the size of the complex. His diagram and his writings are in conflict. Cornuke has falsified the size of the temple in his sketch and relocated the Gihon Spring several hundred feet south of it's actually location.

5). The Staircase from Temple Mount to the Southern City

Josephus describes a stairway leading from the southwest corner of the Temple mount down to the City of David (*Antiquities of the Jews.* XV 11, 5, pg 335). Such a configuration of a stairway is located in the southwestern wall of the traditional Temple mount. Josephus wrote, "Now, in the western

Remains of staircase ledge in wall of Temple mount.

- Google Maps establishes the distance from Gihon Spring to the southern wall of the traditional Temple mount at 804 feet.
- Earnest Martin and his colleagues maintain that the Temple complex as enlarged by Herod was 500 cubits or 750 feet square.
- He also contends that there were two 600 foot bridges extending from the mount down to the Temple complex. Added together the distance is a demanding 1,350 feet.
- Martin asserts that the southeast corner of the Temple complex covered over Gihon Spring making it to be located inside the Temple.
- In reality if you place the southeast corner of the 750 foot Temple complex over Gihon Spring and follow the distance to the north side of the complex, there is only a distance of 54 feet between the Temple complex and the southern wall.
- Taking the more accurate dimension of 20.67 inches per cubit by Leen Ritmeyer, the Temple complex will overlap the southern walls of the traditional mount by 20 feet.

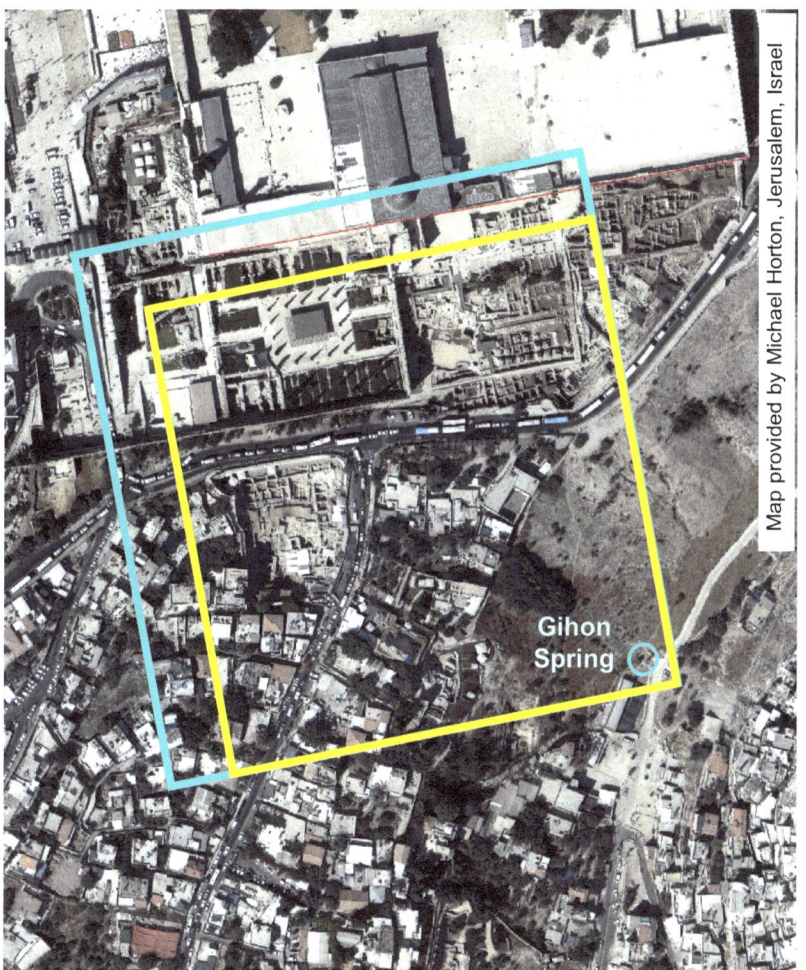

→ The yellow line on this map illustrate the layout of a 750 foot square Temple complex with the southeast corner over Gihon Spring. There are approximately 54 feet left between the Temple complex and the walls of the traditional Temple mount.

→ The blue line represents the more accurate dimension of 861 feet square Temple complex figuring a cubit to be 20.67 inches per cubic. The Temple complex would actually overlap the walls of the traditional site by 57 feet.

→ Earnest Martin claims there were two 600 foot bridges extending from the southwest corner of the Antonia Fortress to the northwest corner of the Temple complex. The actual configuration proves there is **not** room for Martin's alleged layout.

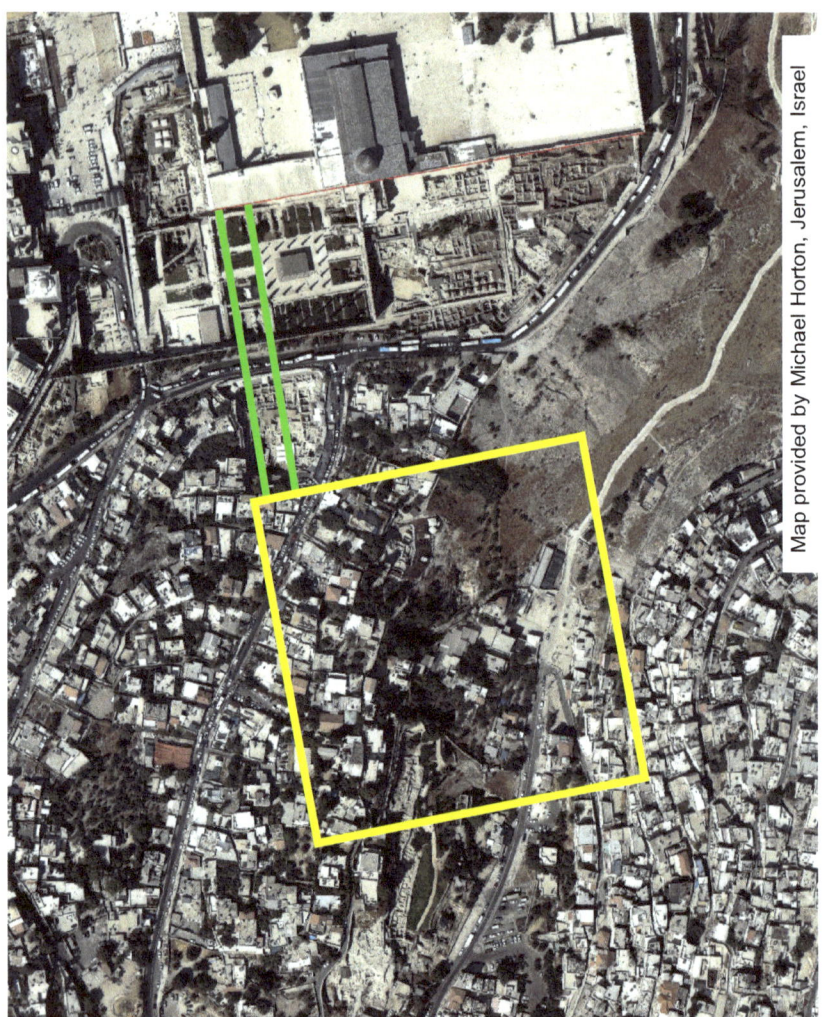

→ This layout reflects exactly what is written in all the books and material by Ernest Martin and his colleagues.
→ It reflects two 600 feet bridges extending from the southwest corner of what they call the Antonia Fortress.
→ It shows a 750 feet square Temple mount at the connection of the bridges at the northwest corner of the Temple complex.
→ Such a layout would cross the Kidron Valley and extend into the Silwan Village. It would completely dam up the water coming down the Kidron Valley creating a large lake and flooding the whole area. It would further extend across the burial tombs in the Silwan area, violating a restriction about building on an unclean site.

Drawing by Leen Ritmeyer

quarter of the enclosures of the temple were were four gates; ... and the last led to the other city, where the road descended down into the valley by a great number of steps and thence up again by the ascent." The remains of such a structure is found on the southwest corner of the traditional Temple mount.

6). The Excavation of the City of David

Had the Temple complex sat in the position as maintained by Ernest Martin and his colleagues, the complex would have totally covered up David's palace and more than half of the city. It would have been necessary, as Ernest Martin claims, to have gone to bedrock to build the massive Temple structure, and that is not the case in the old City of David. The destruction of the city and the Temple would have left much debris throughout the area, yet none has been found. Furthermore, there would not have been room for two bridges each 600 feet long joining the fortress to the City of David. The artifacts relating to the Temple period have been found in the area of the traditional Temple mount and not in the ruins of the City of David.

There is a terraced wall on the eastern side of the City of David that dates back to the time of the Jebusites. Had the massive Temple complex sat above this wall, untold tons of stone and fill dirt would have been required to build up and level the mount in preparation for the foundation of the Temple. Massive walls would have been built on the east and north surrounding the Temple. No evidence of such a construction exists. That is why Martin argued, "It was so destroyed that modern archaeologists will not be able to discover any remnants of it within the confines of its former site. They will not find even its foundation stones that were once strongly positioned in place" (Martin, pg 5). Martin contends the Temple complex was built to bedrock, but previous civilizations are still intact on the bedrock..

7). Garbage Dump In the City of David

In the excavations of the City of David, a Canaanite-era garbage dump has been uncovered. This garbage dump would have been completely covered up by the Temple had it been built in the old City of David. This means the courtyard of the Temple would have covered an "unclean area." Such a placement would have been prohibited by the Law of Moses.

Garbage Dump in the City of David

Across the Kidron Valley into the current Silwan Village were numerous Bronze Age tombs. If the Temple complex had been placed in the City of David, the eastern side would have extended across the valley and sat on top of the burial tombs. This would have rendered the Temple site unclean, in addition to building it on top of a garbage dump.

8). Water for the Temple

Martin, Cornuke, Klein, and Joseph make long arguments that the only source of water for the Temple was Gihon Spring. Gihon Spring was outside the city until King Hezekiah diverted the water through tunnels into the city to the Pool of Siloam. They fail to acknowledge the multiple cisterns and pools of water in and around the Jerusalem.

Underneath the traditional Temple mount were cisterns that held runoff water from the rains. One of the cisterns held more than two million gallons of water. In total, there were some 38 cisterns under the mount built at different times. Outside the mount were dams and channels which contained much water gleaned from the rainfall. The pool known as Bethesda was just one of several pools, some of which have been recently uncovered. At some point in time, an aqueduct was built from pools in Bethlehem all the way to the traditional Temple mount. This aqueduct crossed the Tyropoeon Valley by means of a bridge and onto the mount. The pools and aqueduct would be more than capable of furnishing all the water that the Temple could use.

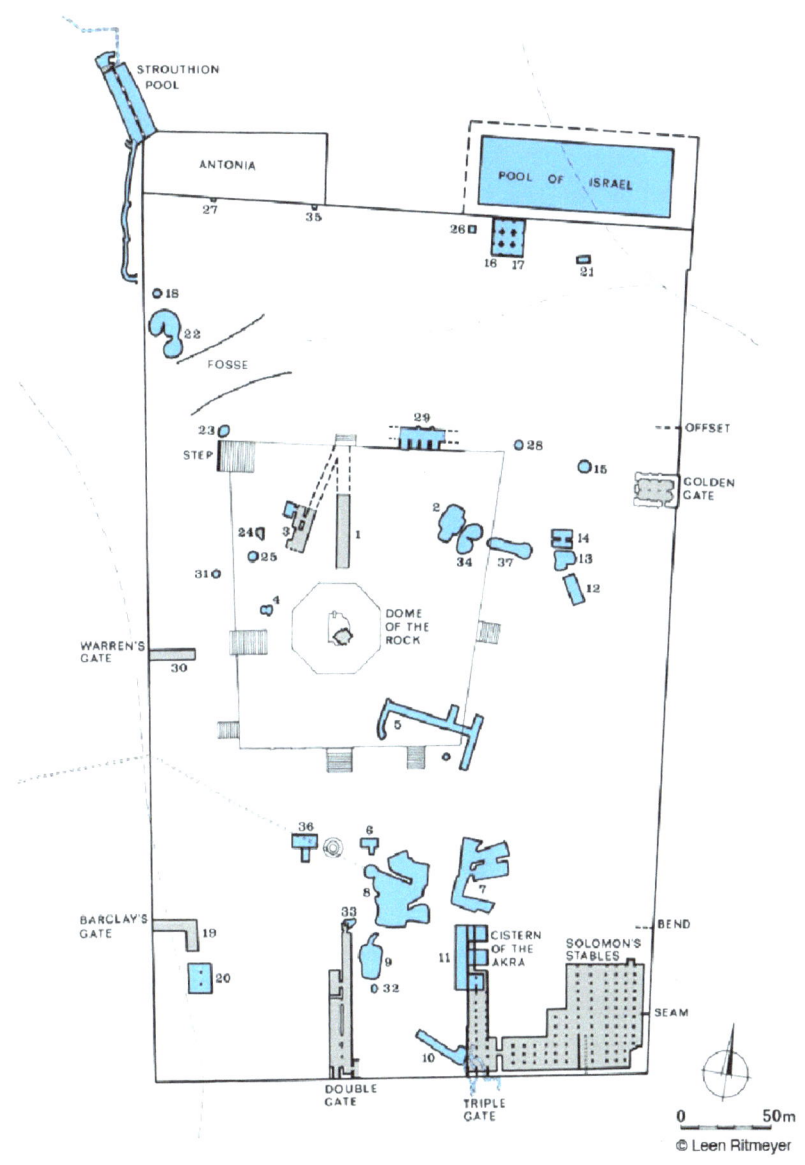

Drawing by Leen Ritmeyer

This diagram reveals the pools of water outside the Temple mount, plus the numerous cisterns underneath. Not included is the aqueduct that came from Bethlehem into the western side that furnished spring water to the Temple. There is a network of channels connecting the various cisterns. One cistern held more than 2 million gallons of water.

A letter written by Aristeas around 250 BC states:

> The Temple faces the east and its back is toward the west. The whole of the floor is paved with stones and slopes down to the appointed places, that water may be conveyed to wash away the blood from the sacrifices, for many thousand beasts are sacrificed there on the feast days. And there is an inexhaustible supply of water, because an abundant natural spring gushes up from within the Temple area. There are moreover wonderful and indescribable cisterns underground, as they pointed out to me, at a distance of five furlongs all around the site of the Temple, and each of them has countless pipes so that different streams converge together.

Other ancient writers confirm that the water source for the Temple was from a cistern rather than the Gihon Spring. "In the chamber of the exile there was a fixed cistern, with a wheel over it, and from there water was provided for all of the courtyard" (*Mishnah Middot* 5, 4, E, pg 883). This chamber was on the south side of the Temple.

9). Mikvah Baths.

Below the traditional Temple mount. and what Martin and his friends call the Antonia Fortress. are multiple mikvah baths both underneath the mount and at all entrances entering it. At the south end of the mount there were two sets of gates, named the double gate and triple gate. Inside those gates before climbing the stairs going to the top, there are mikvah ritual baths where the Jews would wash themselves to become ritually clean in order to proceed into the Temple. If this was a Roman fortress, they would not have allowed such ritual bathing areas.

Mikvah bath at southern steps leading into the Temple Mount

There are additional baths just at the bottom of the steps leading to the Temple Mount. There are baths that have been uncovered in the tunnel project along the Western Wall. One can only conclude that the mount was an area that could be approached only with ritual purity, which would ***not*** be the case if it were merely the Antonia Fortress.

Josephus describes the gates that enter into the southern end of the Temple complex. He stated, "But the fourth front of the temple, which was southward, had indeed itself gates in its middle, as also it had the royal cloisters, with three walks, which reached in length from the east valley unto that on the west" (Antiquities of the Jews, pg 335). It is no coincidence that the southern end of the traditional Temple mount has such gates as described by Josephus, and has in place multiple mikvah baths both outside and inside these gates.

10). The Camp of the Tenth Legion

Martin wrote, "If the Camp of the Tenth Legion had been built in that place, there should be an abundance of artifacts" (Martin, pg 42). Martin's premise is valid. Where the Tenth Legion was camped, there ***would*** be an "abundance of artifacts." Unfortunately, for Martin, there are no Tenth Legion artifacts on the site where he says they were located. His premise is right, but his conclusion is wrong.

Martin and the others wrote their books before the camp of the Tenth Legion was discovered in western Jerusalem. There are no artifacts of the Tenth Legion on the Temple mount, but there are a multitude in an area in western Jerusalem. The camp of the Tenth Legion has been discovered on the Western hill in Jerusalem as the scholars, historians, and archaeologists have always claimed. This fact confirms that Martin, Cornuke, Klein, Joseph, and the others have been very, very wrong.

What's Wrong With This Picture?

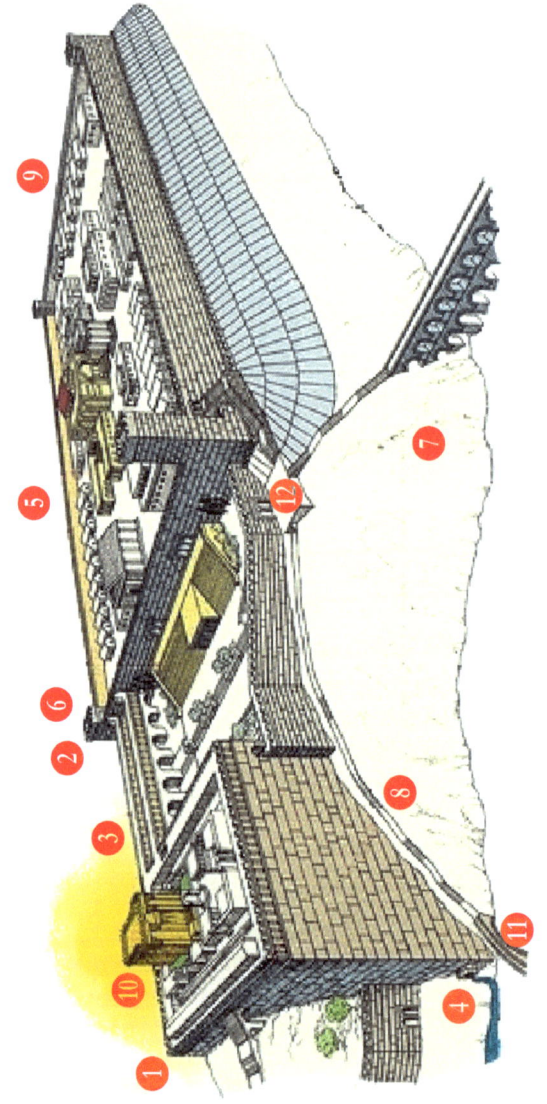

① Josephus wrote that "the place of trumpeting" was located at the southwest corner of the Temple mount. Mr. Martin places the stone here ① However in the ruins following the destruction of Israel, the trumpeting stone was found at the bottom of the debris at the traditional Temple Mount location located here ②.

② In spite of the quotes and claims, there is no historical record in the writings of Josephus and other ancient authors of two bridges connecting the Temple Mount and the Fortress of Antonia.

32

④ It is claimed that the south east corner of the Temple sat over the Gihon Spring, and that the wall stood some 450 feet high. Several issues involved: 1]. The foundation for such a massive wall would have had to be substantial. However, the foundation ruins of a Canaanite tower around the spring are still in place. 2]. If the spring was within the walls of the Temple Complex, why did King Hezekiah dig a tunnel to bring the spring waters "into" the city? 3]. Gihon Spring is in the wrong location on this drawing.

⑤ The complex was remodeled by Herod 105 years before the destruction in AD 70. No Roman Legion was stationed in Jerusalem in the years prior to AD 70. The Tenth Legion arrived in AD 70 to quell the rebellion. The the ruins of the camp of the Tenth Legion along with the artifacts are being excavated in the western part of Jerusalem. There is no archaeological evidence for the camp of the Tenth Legion being on the Temple Mount.

⑥ The eastern gate is missing on the east side as well as the bridge with the aqueduct on the west side. There is no stairway leading down from the southwest corner toward the City of David. Even this complex is incorrectly represented.

⑦ The configuration of the side of the mountain is not realistic. The bridge, the eastern gate, etc. are all figments of the imagination with neither historical or archaeological evidence.

⑧ The complex is out of proportion to the acknowledged claims of Ernest Martin being a square 500 cubits or 750 feet. The drawing is rectangular and greatly subdued to manipulate the temple to fit the location.

⑨ The pattern for the Roman fortress was based on a Roman fortress two centuries later and in a different country.

⑩ Solomon's Temple would have completely covered up and destroyed David's Palace and the major part of the city of David. The city of David encompassed an estimated 12 acres. The 750' square Temple platform encompassed 12.9 acres.

⑪ Martin claims the distance between points (11) and (12) was about 1/4 mile and would include the 600 foot bridges plus the 750 foot Temple complex. The actual distance is approximately 804 feet between Gihon Spring and the southern wall of the Temple Mount. The distance between Warren's shaft and the southern wall is 900 feet. The area is entirely too small to accommodate a 750 foot Temple complex plus 600 foot bridges requiring a distance of 1,350 feet.

Conclusion

I wholeheartedly concur with the comments of David Lazarus in an interview with Eli Shukron, the famed archaeologist of Jerusalem and the City of David, who wrote an article in *Israel Today*, dated 12-13-2019, entitled: "Israeli Archaeologist Debunks Christian Ideas on Temple Mount." Mr. Lazarus' assessment was this:

> Clearly, these Christian 'explorers' are more interested in promoting sensational headlines than learning from the plain facts on the theories, but even worse, makes Christianity and Jesus look foolish in the eyes of prominent Jewish professionals.

Works Cited

Aristeas; *Letter of Aristeas*; First Century BC; R.H. Charles-Editor; Oxford: The Clarendon Press, 1913.

Cornuke, Robert; *Temple*, LifeBridge Books, Charlotte, NC; 2014.

Joseph, Mike M.; *Jerusalem's Temple Mount: The Hoax Of The Millennium*; Author House, Bloomington, IN; 2011.

Josephus, Flavius; Josephus Complete Works; *Antiquities of the Jews, Wars*; Translated by William Whiston; Kregel Publications, Grand Rapids, MI, 1972.

Josephus, Flavius; Josephus II, *The Jewish War*, Books I-III: Translated by H. St. J. Thackeray; Loeb Classical Library; Harvard University Press, London, England; 1989.

Josephus, Flavius; Josephus III, *The Jewish War*, Books IV-VII: Translated by H. St. J. Thackeray; Loeb Classical Library; Harvard University Press, London, England; 1989.

Josephus, Flavius; *The Jewish War,* Translated by Gaalya Cornfeld; Zondervan Publishing House, Grand Rapids, MI; 1982.

Klein, Ken; *Jerusalem And The Lost Temple Of The Jews*; Video Documentary, River Run Productions; 2013.

Lazarus, David; "Israeli Archaeologist Debunks Christian Ideas on Temple Mount," *Israel Today*, Jerusalem, Israel; Dec. 13, 2019.

Martin, Earnest L.; *the Temples that Jerusalem forgot*; Ask Publications, Portland, OR; 2000.

Menachem Davis, ed., *The Book of Psalms,* Mesorah Publications, New York, 2001.

Mishnah, Middot; A New Translation, by Jacob Neusner; Yale University Press, Hamilton Printing Co., Rensselaer, N.Y., 1988.

Ritmeyer, Leen; *The Quest, Revealing The Temple Mount in Jerusalem,* Carta, Jerusalem, Israel, 2006.

Strong's Exhaustive Concordance, Ref. 5001; Power Bible CD; Online Publishing, Inc., Bronson, MI; 2008.

The Holy Bible; King James Version, Cambridge University Press, Great Britain

Other Resources by Dr. Bobby Sparks:

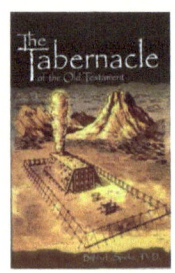

Tabernacle Book
$12.95

13 Session Video Series
including 2 DVDs,
1 Tabernacle Book &
1 Workbook
$99.00

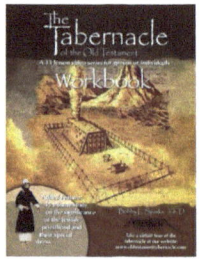

Tabernacle Workbook
$4.95

Priesthood
of Israel
$7.95

Priesthood of Israel
with DVD
$17.95

Was Jesus Crucified on
Wednesday, Thursday, or
Friday?
$4.00

www.oldtestamenttabernacle.com

www.ingramcontent.com/pod-product-compliance
Lightning Source LLC
Chambersburg PA
CBHW041813040426
42450CB00001B/19